M41 WALKER BULLDOG

in action

By Jim Mesko
Color By Don Greer
Illustrated by Perry Manley

Armor Number 29

squadron/signal publications

An M41 Walker Bulldog of the South Vietnamese Army (ARVN) provides covering fire for ARVN troops in Bong Song during the 1972 North Vietnamese Easter Invasion.

ISBN 0-89747-262-4

If you have any photographs of the aircraft, armor, soldiers or ships of any nation, particularly wartime snapshots, why not share them with us and help make Squadron/Signal's books all the more interesting and complete in the future. Any photograph sent to us will be copied and the original returned. The donor will be fully credited for any photos used. Please send them to:

Squadron/Signal Publications, Inc.
1115 Crowley Drive.
Carrollton, TX 75011-5010.

Dedication

This book is dedicated to my wife and parents for all their support during its preparation.

Credits and Acknowledgements

USMC	U.S. Army
NAPCO	FMC
Mike Green	C.F. Foss
J. Wenzl	Michael Jerchel
S. Turnbridge	Armor Magazine
Patton Armor Museum (PAM)	Dave Holt
USAF	MAJ John Montgomery
COL Gordon Kurtz	Greg Beasczad
Austrian Army	MAJ Smock
R.S. Olive	Talbot
GTI	Cadillac Gage

The M41 was the standard U.S. Army light tank during the 1950s and early 1960s, but never saw combat in American service. It was the mainstay of South Vietnamese armored force and served for over a decade. This M41, carrying Vietnamese Marines, moves against anti-government rebel forces near Da Nang during 1966. (USMC)

3

Introduction

During the early days of the Second World War, the basic American light tank was either the M3 or M5 Stuart. Although mechanically sound and a robust performer, the Stuart's light armor and armament severely restricted its employment on the battlefield. Constant requests from field commanders for a better armed and armored vehicle eventually resulted in the introduction of the M24 Chaffee during 1944. With its lightweight, hard hitting 75MM cannon, better armor protection, mechanical reliability and speed, the M24 was probably the finest light tank to see service during the war.

At the end of the Second World War the M24 was the main light tank in service with U.S. armor formations. Although some older model Stuarts were retained for training or to equip Reserve and National Guard formations, most M3/M5s were either scrapped or supplied to various allied forces to rebuild their armored units. Following the war, armchair strategists came to the conclusion that the atomic bomb had made conventional weapons obsolete. Despite such ridiculous theories, which led to massive cuts in conventional defense appropriations, the Army conducted a series of studies on the war to accumulate information and reach some consensus of thought regarding future tactics and weapons employment.

The use of light tanks was one area which was scrutinized and a number of points came out of the study. While prewar doctrine had envisioned that light tanks would be used primarily for scouting, the study concluded that they were rarely used in that role. Instead, they were often used in roles where a heavier main armament was needed. As a result of these findings, the Army realized that any M24 replacement would have to have heavier firepower to deal with the new generation of tanks coming into service with the Russian army. This concern over Soviet armor grew out of fears that the Russians were planning military moves in Europe and other areas as the Cold War heated up during the late 1940s.

Official interest in an M24 replacement began during July 1946 when a new light tank project was initiated under the designation T37. This project called for a vehicle similar in protection and mobility to the M24, but with a more powerful main gun. Weight and size were somewhat restricted because of a desire to have the tank be air-transportable, but this requirement never seriously compromised the overall design since the engineers realized that there were few aircraft at the time capable of hauling such a load. As in the case of the M24 the designers foresaw that the T37 could serve as the bases for a number of related vehicles such as self-propelled artillery, anti-aircraft and armored personnel carriers (APC).

The program engineers envisioned three different turrets, each being more sophisticated than the last. The initial vehicle, designated T37 Phase I, was ready for testing during late 1948. Armed with a 76MM cannon, two .50 caliber machine guns (one coaxial, one pintle mounted for anti-aircraft defense) and two remote controlled 7.62MM machines guns mounted on the turret sides towards the rear, the tank weighed approximately twenty-four tons. The 76MM gun had a steroscope range finder with automatic lead computer and ballistic corrector, polaroid sights, electric turret traverse, and power elevation. Both the hull and turret were of welded construction and power was supplied by a 500 hp Continental gasoline engine. The drum sprocket was located in the rear with the idler wheel in front. There were five road wheels mounted in a torsion bar suspension, along with three return rollers, and a tension roller between the fifth bogey and drive sprocket.

The T37 Phase II version was very similar to the Phase I but featured a completely redesigned turret of both cast and welded construction. An improved T91 76MM gun replaced the earlier armament and a new fire control system was added. A superimposed coincidence range finder coupled to a Vickers stabilization system (in both the vertical and horizontal plane), along with an automatic lead computer replaced the earlier system. This new turret featured a redesigned gun mantlet, less ammunition in a redesigned storage arrangement, and a more angular shape. Supplementary armament remained the same, including the remote controlled machine guns mounted at the turret rear.

The T37 Phase III was envisioned as the combination of the two designs. Using the Phase II as a base, the new vehicle featured an automatic loading 76MM gun and an IBM stabilization system. Otherwise the vehicle was similar to the earlier vehicles.

At the end of World War Two the M24 Chaffee was the standard American light tank, replacing the older M3/M5 Stuart series. Although a robust and mechanically reliable vehicle, its armament was too light to successfully engage new Russian main battle tanks. This fact was graphically demonstrated during the Korean War when the North Korean T-34s dominated the M24s. (PAM)

To replace the M24 a new vehicle was developed using data obtained from an Army study of light tank actions during the war. Designated the T37, this new light tank was to be progressively developed through a series of phases, each being more sophisticated. The first of these, the T37 Phase I had a steroscopic rangefinder which extended out in large bulges on the turret sides. (PAM)

Due to the many differences in the turret design of the T37 Phase II, it was decided to redesignate it the T41. Production of the prototype began and the first vehicle was ready for testing during 1949. One criticism of the T41, which immediately surfaced, was its high cost due to the sophisticated range-finding equipment and various other advanced features. As a result, a new turret was developed which deleted the costly optical system.

This allowed the large range-finder housing to be eliminated, resulting in a much more sleek looking turret. In addition, the remote controlled exterior machine guns were eliminated and the commander's cupola was relocated from the left side to the right side of the turret. This vehicle received the designation T41E1. Later, a hydraulic traverse system was substituted for the electric system, resulting in the T41E2. Testing of both versions progressed with few problems and after reviewing the test results the Army decided to procure the new vehicle under the designation M41.

The revised T37 Phase II/T41 was simplified into the T41E1. The costly and complex optics and range-finder system was deleted, along with the turret bulges. The end product was a much sleeker looking tank with better ballistic protection. The T41E1 was put into production under the designation M41. (PAM)

One of the unique features of the T37 Phase I and II was the remote control .30 caliber machine gun pods mounted on either side of the rear turret. These were deleted on the M41. (U.S. Army)

The T37 Phase II featured a different turret than the Phase I model, being of both welded and cast construction. Both T37s were fitted with two remote controlled .30 caliber machine guns on the turret sides. (PAM)

Army personnel run climbing tests with the T41E2 prototype on the proving ground. Once satisfied with the vehicle, it was put into production as the M41. (U.S. Army)

Development

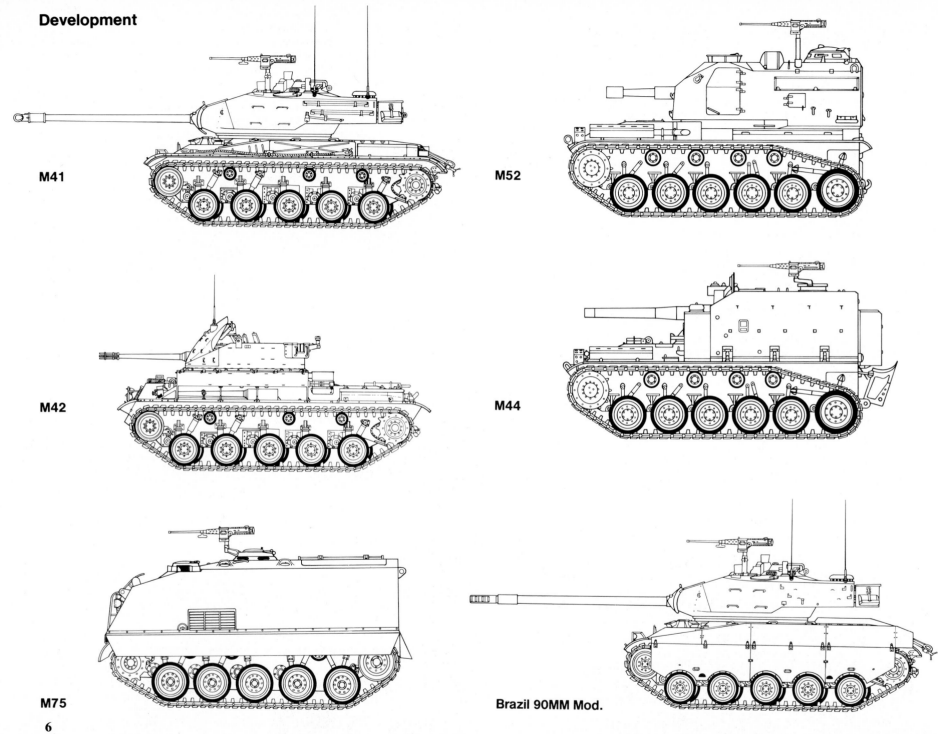

M41

M42

M75

M52

M44

Brazil 90MM Mod.

M41 Walker Bulldog

As a result of increased tensions with the Soviet Union, the U.S. began to rebuild its conventional forces during the late 1940s and early 1950s, particularly after the start of the Korean War (June of 1950). Because testing had progressed smoothly the Army decided to put the T41E1 into production and issued an initial contract for 1,000 vehicles in 1950. As with previous tanks, the T41E1 had received a nickname, the "Little Bulldog," which was a departure from Army practice of naming American tanks after famous generals. This nickname, however, was later amended to the "Walker Bulldog" in honor of GEN Walton Walker, the commander of U.S. forces in Korea who had been killed in a jeep accident during early 1951.

By mid-1951, the first M41s were rolling off the assembly line for issue to armored units. Production of the M41 was undertaken by the Cadillac Motor Car Division of the General Motors Corporation (GMC) at a new production facility in Cleveland, Ohio. This facility, a former aircraft plant, had been used as a storage facility, but was acquired after Cadillac realized its existing facilities in Detroit could not handle production. The plant was renovated and a modern production facility, renamed the Cleveland Tank Arsenal, was set up for the manufacturer of the M41.

The M41 was very conventional in overall design and layout. The hull, of welded construction, was comprised of three sections; the driver's compartment in front, the fighting compartment on the center and the engine housing in the rear. The driver was seated on the left side and access to his area was made through a single hatch, which rotated horizontally to the right. Four periscopes, three facing forward and one facing left, provided acceptable visibility. Steering was done by a control crossbar in combination with the transmission, brakes and accelerator. In case of emergency, an escape hatch was located in the hull under the driver's seat.

The remainder of the crew, the tank commander (TC), gunner and loader were located in the turret which was mounted in the center of the tank. The turret was of both welded and cast construction and had a lightweight sheet metal storage box mounted at the rear. The turret could be traversed 360 degrees in approximately ten seconds and the 76MM gun had a plus 20 degree to minus 10 degree elevation/depression. The TC and gunner were located on the right side of the turret, while the loader was seated on the left side. The commander's cupola was equipped with five vision blocks along with an M20A1 periscope which could be rotated through 360 degrees. The gunner, seated in front of the commander, aimed the 76MM gun through a M97A1 telescopic sight and, in addition, had a M20A1 periscope with 360 degree traverse for observation. The loader, located on the left side, had a single periscope for viewing, although he did have his own hatch to the left and slightly forward of the T.C. Cupola.

The rear compartment housed a six cylinder Continental or Lycoming AOS 895-3 gasoline engine which developed 500 hp at 2,800 RPM. This engine drove the rear mounted sprocket using a GMC CD 500-3 cross-drive transmission which also was linked to the steering mechanism. In case of a fire the compartment was separated from the rest of the tank by a fire-proof bulkhead and was equipped with a fire extinguisher which was operated by the driver. The engine drove a steel track of between 74 to 76 links depending on the model which could be fitted with rubber pads. The M41 had five road wheels, three return rollers, an idler wheel forward, and the drive wheel in the rear. Unlike the early variants, the tension roller between the last bogy wheel and drive sprocket was deleted. Fitted with a torsion bar suspension and hydraulic shock absorbers for the first, second, and fifth bogey wheels, the M41 had a relatively smooth ride over broken ground and its powerful engine and light weight made it an extremely fast and agile vehicle, ideal characteristics for a light tank.

The main armament, an M32 76MM cannon was, at the time, capable of dealing with most Russian armor in service. When newer generation Soviet armor began to appear during the early 1950s, their armor protection resulted in a lessening of the M41's ability to engage them successfully. The gun could fire a wide variety of ammunition, including

There would eventually be four basic M41 variants but externally they were almost impossible to tell apart. This M41A1 differed from the M41 in that it used a hydraulic rather than an electric traverse system to rotate the turret. (PAM)

Workers at the Cleveland Tank Arsenal install a turret in the hull of an M41. During assembly the tank was rolled along the assembly line on its road wheels without the tracks. (PAM)

high explosive (HE), canister, armor piercing (AP), high velocity armor piercing (HVAP), high explosive anti-tank (HEAT), white phosphorus (WP) and training rounds. Additionally, there was a coaxially mounted 7.62MM machine gun to the right of the main gun and a .50 caliber machine gun mounted by the cupola for use by the TC against air or ground targets.

Externally the basic M41 remained the same, although there were four variants. It was almost impossible to differentiate between these variants externally, since the significant changes took place internally. The basic variants and their differences were as follows:

M41: AOS 895-3 engine, electric traverse, M32 76MM cannon, fifty-seven rounds of ammunition

M41A1: AOS 895-3 engine, hydraulic traverse, M32A1 76MM cannon, sixty-five rounds of ammunition, improved fire control equipment.

M41A2: AOS 859-5 engine with fuel injection, similar to M41A1 but with simplified gun/turret controls.

M41A3: similar to M41A2. Earlier variants upgraded with fuel injection kits, could be fitted with infra-red equipment.

Production of the M41 ran until the late 1950s by which time approximately 5,500 vehicles had been manufactured.

The tank commander had five vision blocks and a periscope for observation when the M41 was closed down. The post to the left is the mount for the .50 caliber machine gun which was used for both anti-aircraft protection or close in ground defense. (Mesko)

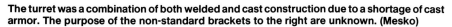

The turret was a combination of both welded and cast construction due to a shortage of cast armor. The purpose of the non-standard brackets to the right are unknown. (Mesko)

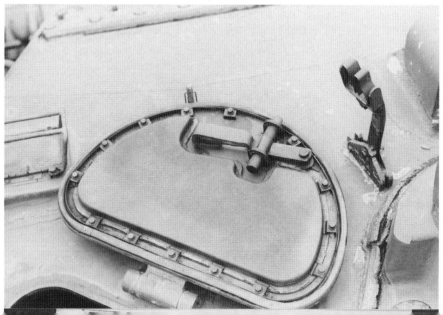

The loader's hatch was to the left and slightly ahead of the commander's cupola. The device next to the hatch was used to secure the barrel of the .50 caliber machine gun when the vehicle was on road march. (Mesko)

Specifications

M41 Walker Bulldog

Crew . . . . Four
Length . . . . .26.9 feet
Height . . . . .8.9 feet
Weight . . . . .51,796 pounds

Armament
Main . . . . .76ᴍᴍ cannon
Secondary . . . . .One .30 caliber coaxial machine
gun, one .50 caliber machine
gun on turret roof.
Engine . . . . .Contential 500 hp
AOS-895-3 gas engine.
Speed . . . . .44.7 mph
Range . . . . .100 miles

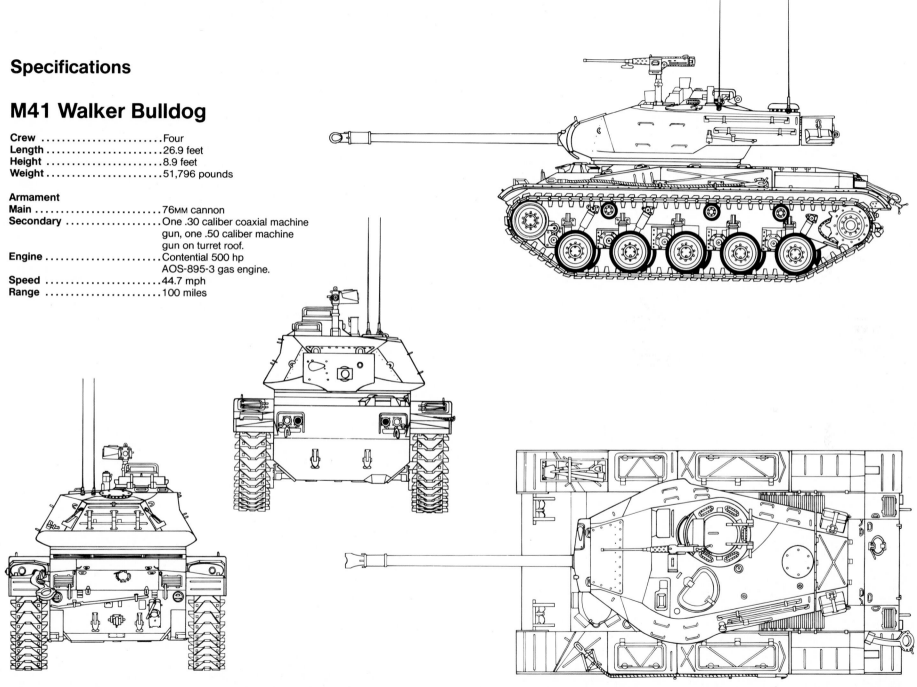

Storage bins were provided on both sides of the hull above the fenders since interior space within the tank was extremely limited and did not allow for the storage of much gear. Additionally, a sheet metal storage bin was attached to the rear of the turret for the crew's personnel effects. (Mesko)

The drive sprockets were located at the rear and drove a 74 to 76 link track. The powerful 500 hp Continental engine gave the M41 a top speed of some 45 miles an hour under good conditions. The cutouts on the inner part of wheel were to reduce weight. (Mesko)

Mufflers were located on both rear fenders. After a short period these gave off a very prominent heat signature and began to glow, making the tank easy to spot at night. To the right of the muffler is the gun barrel travel lock. (Mesko)

The idler wheel in the front had eight holes in each of the wheels to reduce their weight. The track links were fitted with rubber pads and, coupled with the hydraulic shock absorbers and torsion bar suspension, gave the M41 a fairly smooth ride. (Mesko)

An early production M41 being put through its paces by Cleveland Tank Arsenal personnel. The vehicle appears to be fitted with the early style single baffle muzzle brake. (PAM)

Muzzle Brake

M41 (Early)

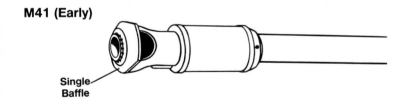

Single Baffle

M41 (Standard)

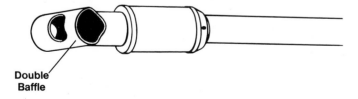

Double Baffle

The M41 had miserable gas mileage and although this was improved with a fuel injected engine, range was never the M41's strong point. As a means of extending the range of early variants four 55 gallon drums were fitted to a special rack at the rear of the hull. These were to be used on road marches and dropped before going into combat. (PAM)

The M41 quickly replaced the M24 Chaffee in frontline service, with many of the vehicles going to Europe. A section of M41s support troops taking part in a training exercise in a built up area. The objects on the front hull appear to be wooden blocks used to prevent the tank from moving while not in use. (PAM)

11

Into Service

During 1953, the M41 began to reach troops in the field to replace their aging M24s. A few were sent to Korea for a combat evaluation, but these saw only limited patrol action in the last days of the war. Based on lessons learned during the Second World War the Army had decided to drop the light tank company from tank battalions and concentrated them in a divisional reconnaissance battalion containing thirty vehicles. Additional light tanks were assigned to each combat command, tank battalion and armored infantry battalion within the division for use in scouting, security and in command/control.

With the end of the Korean War the reorganization of the armored forces became widespread. As production of the M41 began to shift into high gear, the Walker Bulldog quickly superseded the M24 in U.S. service. The bulk of the early M41 production was slated for American armored formations, particularly those in Europe. These units were followed by various Reserve and National Guard units.

By the late 1950s, the M41 had totally replaced the Chaffee. Additional restructuring of the basic armored division resulted in a reduction of total M41 strength during the late 1950s and again in the early 1960s. In the field, the M41 was well liked by its crews. Its handling characteristics, speed, reliability, and small size, were greatly appreciated by the reconnaissance and calvary units, although the noise of the engine was of concern to reconnaissance units. The 76MM gun gave it a useful weapon against most heavier tanks, although its relatively light armor made crews wary of trying to slug it out head to head with heavier tanks. In particular, its small size made it easy to conceal and its combination of light weight and a powerful engine allowed it to go where most medium tanks could not.

Its worst characteristics were its poor mileage (which improved with fuel injected engines), the glow of the exposed muffler covers at the rear (which turned bright red after a little use) and the arrangement of the drivers hatch. This was particularly dangerous since the driver could suffer serious or fatal injuries if the turret was traversed without warning due to the long gun mantlet. These points aside, the "Bulldog" was popular with its crews, who loved to use its high speed to go roaring across fields during maneuvers.

During its service life with the U.S. Army the M41 did not see any significant action. Too late for Korea, it was being replaced by the M551 Sheridan at the time American

This M41 carries the name _"Bulldog"_ on the turret in White. The tank is preparing to conduct a fire mission at Grafenwohr, West Germany, during the Summer of 1955. The main gun of the M41 was able to deal with the Russian T34s but the newer T54/T55 series and the Soviet heavy tanks were far better armored would have been very difficult to deal with for the M41 crews. (U.S. Army)

troops were committed to Vietnam. It did take part in numerous maneuvers, war games and show of force deployments to Thailand during the early 1960s, but this was the limit of its employment in Southeast Asia by American units.

Aside from peace-time use with various armored formations in the U.S. and abroad, the only other action the M41 saw was with some National Guard units who were called up during the civil disturbances which wracked a number of major American cities during the 1960s. During these outbreaks of violence, the M41s were used for crowd control and as cover for infantry units which had to move into sniper controlled areas. In these confrontations, there is no record of the light tanks ever having used their main weapon. By the early 1970s the M41 had been replaced by the M551 Sheridan in all armored formations and the remaining vehicles were either scrapped, used as targets, or supplied to countries with military ties to the U.S.

A lineup of M41s of Company D, 34th Armor during an exercise in the Panama Canal Zone in support of the 20th Infantry during 1960. The M41 operated fairly well in the hot, humid climate, although the crews had to be careful not to overheat the engines. (U.S. Army)

The M41 was used in a variety of climates and proved capable of operating in all types of weather. This M41 was taking part in a training exercise in Alaska during late 1959. The gun is fitted with the more common "T" type muzzle brake. (U.S. Army)

A camouflaged M41 moves up toward a firing range in Alaska in 1961. The vehicle has been field modified with two jerry can holders on the back of the storage bin. Although the M41 could be fitted with side skirts these were rarely seen on operational tanks. (U.S. Army)

Though the M41 could move across country fairly easily, like any tank mud was one of its greatest enemies. This M41 has bogged down during training at Fort Kobblie in the Panama Canal Zone. (U.S. Army)

During 1963, elements of the 25th Infantry Division supported by the 4th Cavalry carried out a road march in Thailand as part of a series of exercises. This M41 is refueled during the exercise, with the gun muzzle covered to keep out moisture. (U.S. Army)

This M41 from C Company, 4th Cavalry took part in maneuvers held in Thailand during the early 1960s. The U.S. did not use the M41 in combat in Vietnam but did provide a number of them to the South Vietnamese during 1965 as part of a massive re-equipment program. (U.S. Army)

The exercises in Thailand tested the ability of the armored and mechanized units to move along the rudimentary road network of the Thai countryside. This small bridge proved able to support the weight of the light tank, much to everyones surprise. (U.S. Army)

When bridges weren't available the tanks had to ford the streams. This M41 created quite a bow wave as it moved across a stream during night maneuvers. (U.S. Army)

An M41 Bulldog pulls a bogged down Thai bus out of the mud during the closing stages of a road march. Such actions helped cement U.S./Thai friendship. This later proved important when Thailand supported the U.S. war effort in Vietnam. (U.S. Army)

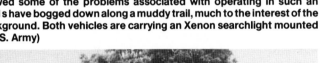

The Thai exercise showed some of the problems associated with operating in such an environment. These M41s have bogged down along a muddy trail, much to the interest of the Thai children in the background. Both vehicles are carrying an Xenon searchlight mounted above the main gun. (U.S. Army)

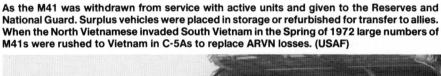

As the M41 was withdrawn from service with active units and given to the Reserves and National Guard. Surplus vehicles were placed in storage or refurbished for transfer to allies. When the North Vietnamese invaded South Vietnam in the Spring of 1972 large numbers of M41s were rushed to Vietnam in C-5As to replace ARVN losses. (USAF)

15

M42 Duster

The chassis of the M41 was intended, as had been the case with the M24, to serve as the basis for a series of related vehicles. Development of an anti-aircraft vehicle designated the T141 began during 1950 using a modified M41 chassis. While the rear portion remained virtually unchanged, the forward two thirds was extensively rebuilt. A large crew compartment was added for the driver and an assistant driver, entry to which was gained through a large hatch on the front glacis plate or through two hatches on the hull top. In the vehicle center, a new turret ring was added to hold a revolving gun tub armed with twin 40MM Bofors automatic cannons. This gun tub was basically the same one used on the M19, with various modifications to improve its performance. On either side of the turret, ammunition boxes and storage points for extra barrels and other equipment were added.

Following testing of the prototype, production of the vehicle, under the designation M42 "Duster," was begun during 1953. The M42 was powered by the same 500 hp AOS-895-3 Continental engine used in the M41/M41A1 which gave miserable gas mileage. During 1956, the improved AOS-895-5 with fuel injection was substituted for the AOS-895-3 engine which helped increase the vehicle's range. These "Dusters" were designated the M42A1.

The main armament of the M42, was a license built Swedish 40MM Bofors cannon. This was an excellent anti-aircraft weapon which had proved its worth in both World War Two and Korea, though in the latter conflict it had been used almost exclusively in the ground support role. Capable of firing 240 rounds per minute with a variety of fuses, the guns were equipped with conventional optics for target acquisition.

The T141 was part of a program to upgrade the mobile anti-aircraft protection of the armor forces. The T141 was basically an M41 hull fitted with the turret from the M19. The T141 was deemed an improvement over the M19 and was placed in production as the M42. This T141 was engaged in early testing of the vehicle during the early 1950s. (PAM)

M19

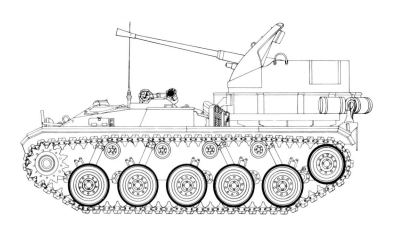

Improved optics, along with the fuel injected engine, were used in the M42A1. The guns were hand loaded with four round clips, 100 clips being carried in ready access storage boxes on the vehicle hull. Several different fire control radars were developed for possible use with the M42 by both Lockheed and Sperry but these were never put into service. This lack of radar meant that the M42 could only be effectively used in relatively clear weather against slow moving targets. Though the guns had an effective range of 3.5 miles, the "Duster" was of little value against high speed aircraft and, as the Soviet Union began to field a new generation of jet ground support aircraft, the effectiveness of the M42 declined sharply.

As with the M41 series, the M42 was produced by the Cadillac Division of G.M.C. When production terminated in the late 1950s, approximately 3,700 units had been manufactured. These equipped the self-propelled anti-aircraft units in the various Army air defense units, replacing the M19 and various half track mounted weapons. Eventually, they were also issued to Reserve and National Guard units, along with numerous foreign countries under the Military Assistance Program.

By the late 1960s, the limits of the M42 were evident and a replacement for it, the M163 Vulcan, began being issued to the armored units. Three battalions, however, were shipped to Vietnam, where a lack of enemy aircraft led to their use in perimeter defense, base security and as convoy escorts. Their high rate of fire and projectile weight proved to be very effective in suppressing enemy fire in the dense jungle conditions. It was not unusual to see scores of four round clips wedged in and around a Duster turret during a fire mission in order to provide a high volume of fire. Many M42s in Vietnam had the flash suppressors removed from the gun barrels. Additionally, most had their secondary armament changed from the M1918 .30 caliber machine gun to the M60 7.62MM machine gun. Eventually, the South Vietnamese Army also received Dusters and these were used in much the same way, right up to the fall of Saigon in 1975.

Other than its use in Vietnam, the M42 saw little combat service, except in the Middle East where they were employed by the Jordanians against the Israelis during the 1967, Six Day War. It is believed that some were used in Lebanon during the early days of its civil war. In the U.S., the arrival of its replacement relegated the Duster to various Reserve and National Guard units. Gradually, even these formations began to re-equip and, by the late 1980s, only three National Guard units were still using the vehicle. These were finally phased out and during 1990, all three units began to receive replacement vehicles, closing out over thirty-five years of service in the U.S. inventory.

Access to the hull was through a large door on the hull front or through the two hatches in front of the gun turret. While the open topped turret provided easy access to the gun the lack of overhead cover was a serious problem in a combat zone since the crew lacked protection from shrapnel and small arms fire. (PAM)

This M42 has its guns at full elevation, (85° when on power drive, 87° using the manual mode). The turret could traverse a compete 360° and if needed in the ground support role the guns could be depressed to -5°, a feature which later proved valuable in Vietnam. (Montgomery via Kurtz)

The forward two thirds of the M41 hull was redesigned to accept the M19 turret, while the engine deck remained basically the same. Storage boxes for ammunition, spare gun barrels and other gear were provided on top the fenders on both sides of the turret. For close-in defense a .30 caliber machine gun was carried on the turret. (PAM)

17

Specifications

M42 Duster

Crew ....Six
Length ....20.8 feet
Width ....10.5 feet
Height ....9.3 feet
Weight ....49,497 pounds

Armament
Main ....Two 40MM Bofors cannon.
Secondary ....One .30 caliber machine gun
or one M60 7.62MM
Engine ....One Continental 500 hp
AOS-895-3 gas engine.
Speed ....45 mph
Range ....100 miles

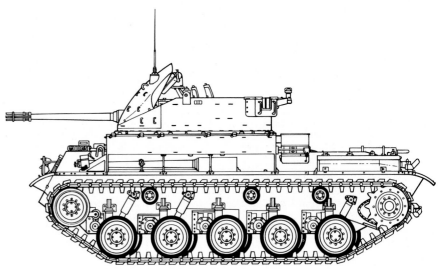

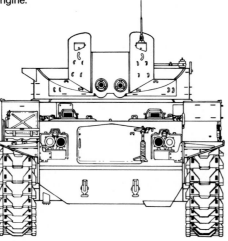

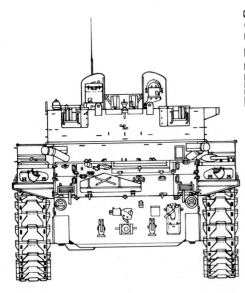

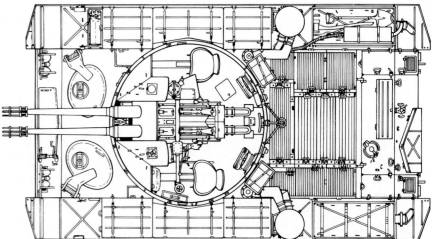

Access to the hull was through a large door which opened to the left with the aid of a large coiled spring. The gun barrels were fitted with three pronged flash suppressors. (Montgomery via Kurtz)

The vehicle commander sat on the right side of the M42. The upright frame could be quickly detached at the top and moved forward to allow access to the storage compartment behind it. The height of the seat could only be adjusted with no one sitting in it. (Montgomery via Kurtz)

The driver sits on the left of the vehicle and steered the Duster using the control crossbar. The small device with the "T" handle is the range selector control lever for neutral park, neutral steer, low, high, and reverse gear ranges. (Montgomery via Kurtz)

Unlike the commander's seat, the driver's seat can only be adjusted for height with the driver sitting in it. The small warning sign reads *Warning: High Intensity Noise, Hearing Protection Required.* (Montgomery via Kurtz)

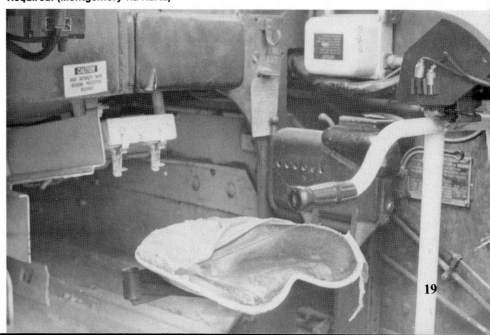

19

The gun turret of this M42 is traversed to the rear. On the outside of the turret are mounts for machine guns, ready boxes to store ammunition and over forty tie downs to hold gear or camouflage material. (Montgomery via Kurtz)

The M38 Computing Sight was located on the right side of the gun. The knob on the left is the speed knob, while the one on the right is the computer bail. The wheel at the bottom of the M38 is the computer positioning handwheel. (Montgomery via Kurtz)

Empty shell casings were ejected out the rear of the gun mount into these chutes located underneath the guns on the vehicle floor. During periods of rapid fire the floor quickly became cluttered with shell casings. (Montgomery via Kurtz)

The M42 was loaded with four round clips which were inserted into the automatic loader visible here in the middle of the gun top. The guide chutes for the ammunition clips are located in front and behind the automatic loader. (Montgomery via Kurtz)

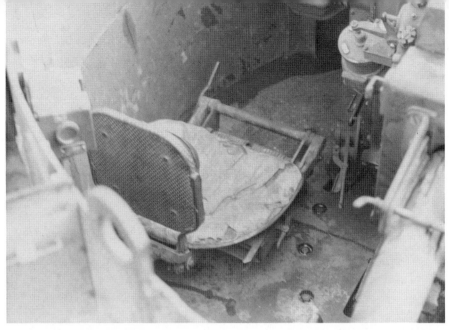

The gunner's seat was located on the left side of the guns while the lead setter sat on the right side. To adjust the seat's height it was necessary to be sitting in it. (Montgomery via Kurtz)

The rear decking, aside from the air cleaners and exhausts, was very similar to the M41. The center grate (below the gun barrels) covers the engine air cleaner. (Montgomery via Kurtz)

Access to the engine area was good because of the multiple access hatches. When the newer fuel injected A0S-895-5 engine was substituted for the earlier power plant the modified Dusters were redesignated as M42A1s. (Montgomery via Kurtz)

From the ground, maintenance on the engine was fairly easy unless a total overhaul was needed, since most engine parts were within arms reach. The tubes going out to either side from the engine are the exhausts. (Montgomery via Kurtz)

21

There were two large drum shaped air filters carried above the fenders in front of the mufflers. These helped cut down on dust and dirt getting into the engine and causing excessive wear on engine parts. (Montgomery via Kurtz)

The exhausts were similar to those used on the M41 except for the guard around them. These guards were also used to store track links and tools. An auxiliary muffler was located over the top of the right muffler. The mufflers would glow Red after a few hours of operation, like those on the M41. (Montgomery via Kurtz)

The auxiliary muffler on top the right muffler took up some of the space formerly used for tool storage. Extreme care was needed when the vehicle was operating so that the crew did not touch or store gear near the hot muffler surface. (Montgomery via Kurtz)

The vehicle identification markings above the headlight are on a Buff colored background which allowed for quick vehicle identification but did not stand out for the enemy to locate. This vehicle was used by Ohio National Guard which operated M42s until 1990. (Motgomery via Kurtz)

The M42 quickly replaced the M19 in the mobile anti-aircraft role. Until the advent of specialized jet ground attack aircraft and helicopter gunships, the vehicle provided useful service in the air defense role. (PAM)

Though never really used in the air defense role the M42 did see service in Vietnam as a fire support vehicle and convoy escort. With a high rate of fire and heavy projectile they proved to be very effective in the dense jungles. This Duster moves through Tay Ninh on Highway 26 during convoy escort armed with two M60 machine guns for close-in defense. (U.S. Army)

Flash Suppressor

M42   Three Fork
Flash Suppressor

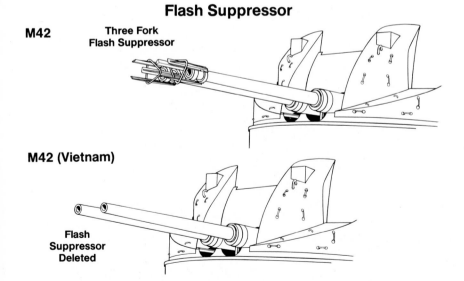

M42 (Vietnam)

Flash
Suppressor
Deleted

(Right) Often the M42s on perimeter defense were dug into prepared positions with only their turrets above ground level. This vehicle is being moved into such a position in support of U.S. Marines near the DMZ during the Summer of 1967.

Duster crews usually stacked the turret ring and storage boxes full of four round forty millimeter clips for easy access during a fire support mission. The twin cannons had a high rate of fire and the crews could easily use up large quantities of ammunition within a few minutes. (PAM)

This M42 takes part in Operation *Pershing* in support of the 1st Battalion, 7th Regiment, 1st Cavalry Division. The Dusters were often used to supplement tanks and APCs in the ground support role. Unfortunately their open top and high silhouette made them susceptible to small arms fire, grenades, and RPGs. (U.S. Army)

A pair of M42s pass an M113 of the 1st Battalion, 50th Mechanized Infantry on their way to LZ *Sandy*. The rear vehicle carries two M60 machine guns on the turret gun mounts, a common practice in Vietnam, where the crews added as much firepower to their vehicles as possible. (U.S. Army)

The crew of this M42 of D Battery, 5th Battalion, 2nd Artillery, have improvised a sun shield using poles and part of a tent. The hot tropical sun in Vietnam could make metal almost too hot to handle. During the monsoon season such a shield also helped keep moisture off the guns though rust was always a problem. (U.S. Army)

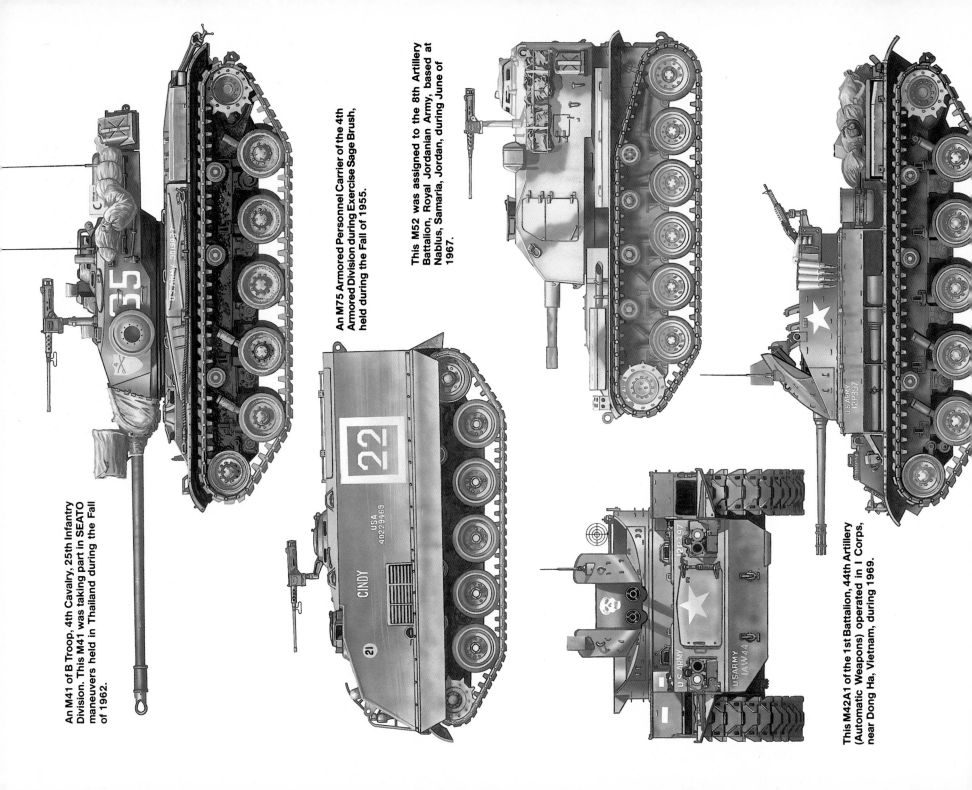

An M41 of B Troop, 4th Cavalry, 25th Infantry Division. This M41 was taking part in SEATO maneuvers held in Thailand during the Fall of 1962.

An M75 Armored Personnel Carrier of the 4th Armored Division during Exercise Sage Brush, held during the Fall of 1955.

This M52 was assigned to the 8th Artillery Battalion, Royal Jordanian Army, based at Nablus, Samaria, Jordan, during June of 1967.

This M42A1 of the 1st Battalion, 44th Artillery (Automatic Weapons) operated in I Corps, near Dong Ha, Vietnam, during 1969.

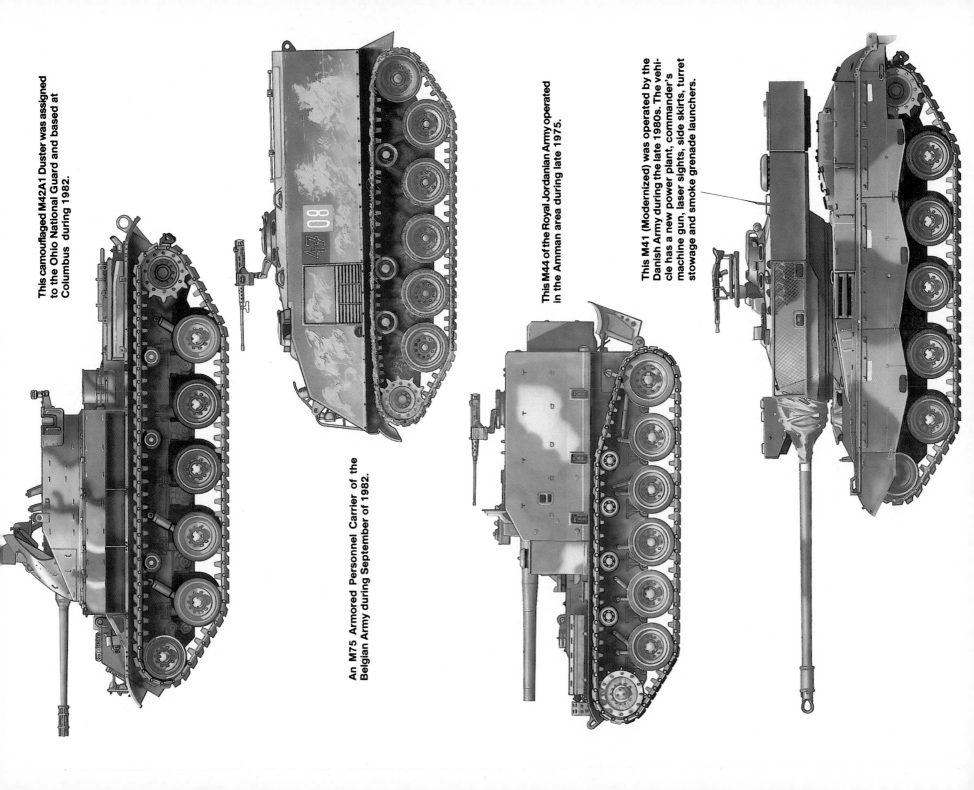

This camouflaged M42A1 Duster was assigned to the Ohio National Guard and based at Columbus during 1982.

An M75 Armored Personnel Carrier of the Belgian Army during September of 1982.

This M44 of the Royal Jordanian Army operated in the Amman area during late 1975.

This M41 (Modernized) was operated by the Danish Army during the late 1980s. The vehicle has a new power plant, commander's machine gun, laser sights, side skirts, turret stowage and smoke grenade launchers.

The South Vietnamese also used the M42 during the later stages of the war. This ARVN vehicle was positioned alongside a road during the initial stages of the North Vietnamese 1972 Easter Invasion, Although the M42 could easily defeat lightly armored and softskinned NVA vehicles, it had little effect on the heavily armored T34s, T54s and T59s. (U.S. Army)

A large number of foreign countries also received M42s as part of American military aid programs. These Lebanese Dusters take part in a parade prior to the outbreak of the Lebanese Civil War which began during the early 1970s. There has been no information about the use of the M42s by the various warring factions. (PAM)

In addition to the M41, neutral Austria also received a number of M42s. These very clean and well maintained M42s took part in a military parade in Vienna. (Wenzl via Jerchel)

M75

During the Second World War, the standard armored personnel carrier (APC) was the M3 half track, an open topped vehicle built on a truck type chassis with a tracked suspension in the rear. Toward the end of the war steps were taken to develop a fully tracked and enclosed APC based on the M18 Tank Destroyer and M24 Light tank. These programs resulted in the M39 and M44. Although a step in the right direction, both vehicles exhibited serious shortcomings and, following the end of the war, the army began work on a replacement vehicle.

This vehicle was intended to correct the more serious shortcomings of the M44, which included a better troop exit, a lower silhouette, better protection and lower weight. The new design was based on the T43 cargo carrier, then under development, which shared many components with the T41 tank. Designated T18, the prototype was ready for testing during late 1950. Somewhat similar in appearance to the M44, the T18 was substantially lighter in weight and smaller in overall size. The engine was mounted in the forward portion of the starboard hull and was attached to a series of rollers for easy removal. The driver was seated to the left of the engine while the commander sat in the middle of the hull behind the engine. The troop compartment was behind the commander with seats for eleven infantrymen. The troops could exit the T18 through two large rear doors or through two roof hatches.

Vision for the driver and commander was adequate, the former having three periscopes, while the latter had a cupola with several vision ports. Unfortunately, vision for the troops was limited to opening the roof hatches, an impractical approach if the vehicle was under fire. This lack of vision ports led to a feeling of claustrophobia for the infantry in the rear. Additionally, when they exited the vehicle they wasted precious time getting oriented to the terrain, which in a combat situation could be crucial.

Originally the T18 was not armed but early in the testing program a remote controlled .50 caliber machine gun was fitted to the commander's cupola. Following this, provisions were made for two remotely controlled .30 or .50 caliber machine guns in boxes on either side of the commander's position. These were electro-hydraulically controlled, had three sights for target acquisition and rotated through an arc of 220 degrees. Each turret could be controlled from any sight station and both could be brought on target simultaneously. In the T18E1, this system was replaced by a remote controlled turret with twin .50 caliber machine guns mounted over the commander's position. This was later replaced by a single machine gun. Later, in the T18E2, the turret reappeared. Finally, the production vehicle reverted to a single pintle mounted .50 caliber machine gun on the commander's cupola.

Testing of the various prototypes continued during the early 1950s and, in December of 1952, the T18E1 was declared ready for Army service. Aside from armament differences and minor details, the most significant difference between the two versions were the top hatch arrangement and the addition of an exhaust pipe across the front of the hull on the T18E1. Full scale production began immediately under the designation M75 and ran until early 1954, with 1,729 vehicles being produced by International Harvester and F.M.C. The only significant difference in production vehicles were in louver size (narrow versus coarse), top armor protection (9.5 mm versus 12.7m) and engine door handle arrangement on the right side.

The M75 quickly replaced the M44 most notably in European based units, where it took part in extensive maneuvers to test its reliability in the field. Although a definite improvement over the M44, its main drawbacks were its size, high cost, exposed engine grills and it was not amphibious. By the late 1950s, a newer APC, the M59 from FMC had begun to replace it and most of the remaining vehicles were turned over to Belgium. The Belgian Army used the vehicle well into the 1980s before replacing it with another FMC built APC, the M113.

To replace the heavier and larger M44 the Army developed a new APC based on the T43 cargo carrier which used many of the components of the M41. Designated the T18, the vehicle was a major improvement, being better protected, lighter, smaller and having superior troop exit facilities. This T18 was the first pilot model of the project. (PAM)

Various armament configurations were tried on the early prototypes. One of the more unusual configurations being dual remote controlled machine gun turrets, which could be sighted from a number of stations. These proved impractical, however, and were never adopted. (PAM)

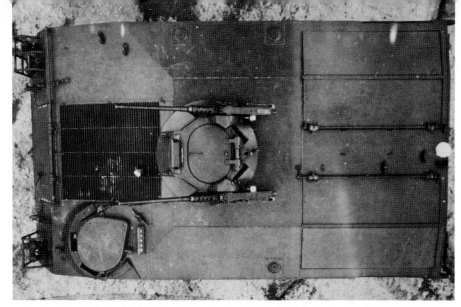

Another armament configuration was a turret on top the commander's hatch which carried twin .50 caliber machine guns. This system would also be tried on later models, but was never put into production. (PAM)

Exhaust louvers were located on either side of the hull in addition to the exhaust outlet on the forward front hull. These were considered a weak point in the overall design of the vehicle since they were open to enemy fire. This T18E1 was fitted with a single .50 caliber machine gun mounted on a new commander's cupola. This later became standard on production vehicles. (FMC via Green)

Experimental M75 Variants

Some thought had been given to producing different mortar variants of the basic M75 to support troops in the field. These included the T62 (81MM mortar), T63 (105MM mortar) and T64 (4.2 inch mortar). Each vehicle was very similar to the others, with the rear top armor being removed to facilitate weapon clearance and crew service. By the time the prototypes were ready for testing, the M59 was almost ready to enter production and the decision was made to concentrate on its chassis since it was superior in all respects to the M75.

Some changes were also tried on the basic M75 to improve its general performance. One vehicle was modified with larger bogey wheels and no return rollers to improve ride and cross-country mobility. Designated M75 (Flat Suspension) it did little to improve the basic vehicle and warranted no change in the production model. Another version received a more streamlined body to improve armor protection and reduce weight. This vehicle, the T73, was somewhat better than the M75, but there was not enough improvement to justify its introduction onto the production line, particularly with production beginning on the superior M59.

An improved version, the T18E1, differed from the T18 in having a different hatch arrangement and an exhaust pipe across the front of the vehicle. This T18E1 is fitted with a dome mount carrying a .30 caliber machine gun. (PAM)

Eventually the T18E1 was standardized as the M75 and put into production during the late 1950s. The large exit doors at the rear provided easy entry for the soldiers inside. Later models of the M75 would have slightly different door locks, louvers and the handle on the forward engine access door would be simplified. (PAM)

The M75 saw only limited service with U.S. troops before being replaced by the M59. The majority of M75s eventually ended up with the Belgium Army or on gunnery ranges. This group of GIs are briefed on the characteristics of the vehicle by their squad leader. (PAM)

The T64 carried a large number of rounds for the mortar in the weapons bay area but the lack of overhead protection would have been a serious handicap in combat. A ground mount for the mortar was carried on the top left side of the hull and on the right front glacis plate. (PAM)

Suspension

M75 (Early)

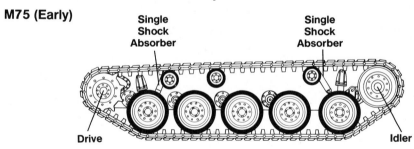

Single Shock Absorber

Single Shock Absorber

Drive

Idler

M75 (Late)

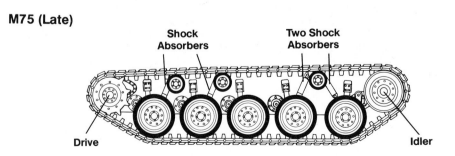

Shock Absorbers

Two Shock Absorbers

Drive

Idler

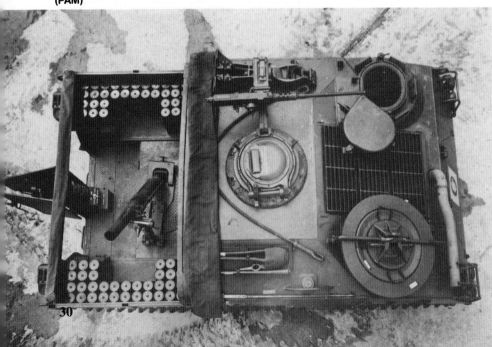

M52

The M52 was one of the two self-propelled (SP) artillery pieces based on M41 components, both of which were designed to replace the 105MM M37 which had been based on the M24 light tank. Work began on the design during the late 1940s under the designation T98. To overcome the problems associated with the limited traverse of Second World War SP guns, the 105MM cannon of the T98 was mounted in an armored turret. Originally it was intended to use a "state of the art" or "ultimate" fire control system but numerous problems led to the adoption of a simpler, less complicated and mechanically more reliable system.

The T98 was a light self-propelled howitzer mounting a 105MM cannon in a revolving turret which was mounted on the rear of the vehicle with the engine in the front. Secondary armament consisted of a .50 caliber machine gun on the commander's cupola. (PAM)

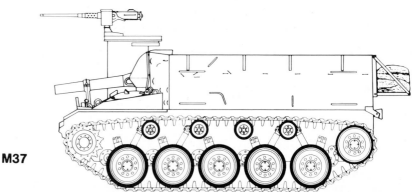

M37

U.S.A.
40227061

Unlike the M41, the T98 had its overall arrangement reversed, with the turret mounted toward the back and the engine up front. The first prototype of the T98 was ready for testing during early 1950 but changes in the T41 (M41) program resulted in delays. Due to the onset of the Korean War the test period for T98 was cut short and the vehicle, redesignated the M52, was rushed into service. As a result major problems arose with production vehicles, leading to a series of costly modifications which delayed service introduction of the M52 until 1955.

The production vehicle mounted an M49 105MM cannon in a revolving turret with 105 rounds stowed in the vehicle. In addition to the main gun, the M52 was also equipped with a .50 caliber machine gun for anti-aircraft and close-in defense. The machine gun was mounted on the commander's hatch on the right side of the turret top. The gunner was located in front of him while the driver sat on the other side of 105MM gun. The remainder of the crew was located in the rear of the turret. As with other vehicles of this era, the M52 had poor gas mileage. With the development of the fuel injected engine, later production vehicles were fitted with this power plant in place of the original Continental or Lycoming AOS 895 engine. These were designated M52A1s and also incorporated minor changes in the fire control system.

Production ran from the mid to late 1950s, with a total of 684 vehicles coming off the assembly line. These were used to equip numerous light self-propelled artillery battalions and artillery units in Austria, West Germany, Spain and Jordan, where it saw action in the 1967 Arab-Israeli War.

With newer, more capable vehicles coming into the inventory, the M52 had only a relatively short service life with U.S. forces and was quickly replaced with the more potent M108/M109 series of vehicles.

Provisions were made for the T98 to ford fairly deep water using a watertight sealing kit and muffler extensions. This equipment was rarely, if ever, used in actual service. (PAM)

The enclosed turret provided a degree of protection from shrapnel though it was unable to stop any type of hit from a high velocity weapon. The fixtures on the starboard side are used to hold spare track links while the access plate on the port side allowed the crew to carry out maintenance on the gun elevation mechanism. (PAM)

Access to the turret and rear hull was gained through a number of large doors. These doors opened in different directions, and some doubled as platforms. The prototype vehicles used different tracks than the production variant. (PAM)

The engine compartment on the T98E1 was modified substantially with a different grill arrangement and a revised rear decking. This vehicle was fitted with the type of track used on the production M52. (PAM)

The right side of the turret differed greatly from the port side both in general outline and shape. Additionally, the storage brackets varied and there was no large access hatch for crew entry. Muffler arrangement was similar on both sides. Production vehicles would later have an extra return roller added to the suspension. (PAM)

Changes in the prototype resulted in the T98E1 which featured a number of changes in the general turret outline, an additional return roller, a slightly different muffler arrangement and internal engine changes. (PAM)

The turret of the M52 was cramped and crowded. The device on the left side was a rack for shells which rotated, allowing the crew to select the proper type of round needed for a particular fire mission. (PAM)

The M52 saw only limited service with U.S. forces before being replaced with newer self-propelled guns. The M52 did see some combat service with the Jordanian Army and a number were captured by the Israeli Army during the 1967 Six Day War. (PAM)

An early T98E1 being put through cold weather tests in the early 1950s. The rush to get the vehicle into service resulted in numerous problem in the production vehicle, which could have been found and fixed under a more regular test program. (PAM)

Suspension

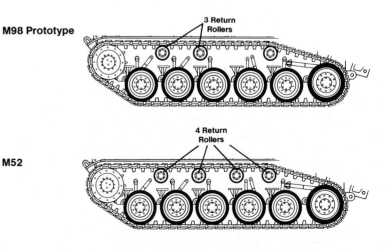

M98 Prototype

3 Return Rollers

M52

4 Return Rollers

34

M44

The replacement for the 155MM M4 self-propelled howitzer was the T99, which generally resembled the M52 in overall appearance. The 155MM cannon was mounted in a turret at the rear of the vehicle to overcome the limited traverse of the M41 SPH. As with other vehicles developed at this time, prototype testing was cut short and the T99 was rushed into production before all the bugs were worked out.

This decision proved to be ill-advised as various problems with the fire control system, turret, and other technical shortcomings resulted in a vehicle which was unable to function in its assigned role properly. After an initial production run of 250 vehicles it was decided to modify the basic design and do away with the turret. This new design, designated the T194, featured a barbette type mount for the 155MM gun and eliminated the overhead armor. The redesign solved the major problems which had cropped up in the T99 and production was reinstated with this derivative, under the designation M44.

The earlier T99s were returned to the factory and rebuilt to this new configuration. When production was completed during the late 1950, slightly over 600 vehicles had been completed, including the rebuilt vehicles and others fitted with a more fuel efficient engine, designated M44A1.

The M44 saw only limited service with U.S. forces, being quickly replaced by more advanced vehicles. Many were supplied under military aid programs to various NATO countries including Belgium, Germany, Italy, France, Great Britain, and other recipients including Spain and Jordan, who used them in action against Israel during the 1967 Six Day War. The Jordanian Army lost a sizeable number of these vehicles to the Israeli Army during its drive to the Jordan River. These were not put into Israeli service and were probably sold on the international arms market or used as targets. As late as the mid-1970s Jordan still fielded a force of around twenty M44s, but these probably have since been replaced by more modern vehicles.

The T99E1 prototype had overhead armor protection which was deleted on later production vehicles. When the armored top was deleted, the rear doors were modified. (PAM)

Like the T98 the T99 program suffered many problems because of the rush to get the vehicle into service. The initial vehicles were fitted with overhead armor but this was later deleted. This T99E1 has a modified engine deck similar to the T98E1. (PAM)

Problems with the enclosed turret led to a major rebuild program intended to make the vehicle suitable for use in the field. The armored top was removed and cover from the elements was provided by a removable canvas tarp. Various changes were also made to the superstructure due to these changes. (PAM)

The redesigned vehicle mounted the 155MM gun in a limited traverse casemate which severely restricted its movement. Additionally the lack of overhead protection exposed the crew to enemy fire and the elements. (Mesko)

An early vehicle being put through field tests. The changes in the vehicle resulted in a change in designation from T99 to T194, with production models receiving the designation M44. These saw only limited service in the U.S. Army before being phased out in the early 1960s. (PAM)

The eventual replacement for the M52/M44 series was the M108/M109 series of self-propelled guns. The M108 mounted a 105MM gun while this M109 carried a 155MM gun. (U.S. Army)

36

QM41

One of the most interesting variants of the M41 family was the QM 41, a remote controlled converted tank ordered by the U.S. Navy for use in testing air-to-ground missiles. The major conversion work involved the removal of the turret and its replacement by a half inch steel dome to provide fragmentation protection. Mounted on top the dome was a small platform which served as a support for a series of high intensity lights. These included a clear light for visual sighting and locating purposes, a red light for signaling either engine, electrical, or radio malfunction and a blue light for speed indication.

Additionally, there were provisions for a radio antenna, a rear facing road lamp and a circular hatch located on the port side of the dome, toward the rear. The dome was painted a distinct pattern, the starboard side being White and the port side being Red, to aid in visual identification.

Control of the QM 41 was either by manual or remote control. A screen was placed over the driver's periscope blocks to provide protection for the glass from flying debris during testing. When operating under manual control, the crew consisted of one man (a driver).

The QM 41 was used by the Navy at its southwest U.S. test ranges for a number of years to test various types of air-to-ground ordnance, particularly the early generations of laser guided or "smart" weapons. The exact number of units produced is unknown, but it is believed that it was relatively small. The QM 41 was also used during the initial development and testing of the M551 Sheridan turret. It is believed that the vehicles were retired from service during the early 1970s, although at least one still survives in storage at the Patton Armor Museum.

The basic hull was modified very little aside from moving the small auxiliary muffler to the right front fender and providing additional protection for the driver's vision ports. (PAM)

The QM41 was a specially modified M41 used by the U.S. Navy as a mobile test platform for air-to-ground weapons. The turret was replaced by an oval dome which mounted a series of lights which enabled the pilots to determine the location and the direction in which the vehicle was moving along with its status. (PAM)

The various beacons carried by the QM41 were mounted on a small platform on top of the dome. These beacons provided a series of visual signals indicating location, direction of travel, and status of the vehicle. The perforated plates in front of the drivers vision ports provided protection from flying debris and shrapnel. (Bieasczad)

37

Experimental Variants

In addition to the vehicles which were produced in quantity, there were also a number of variants of the M41 design which never progressed beyond the prototype stage. Two of these were designed to supplement the M42 in the anti-aircraft role. A T18 automatic 75MM cannon was fitted on the rear of a modified M41 hull for field testing, similar to a conversion tried earlier on the M24 Chaffee. The gun mount had no armor protection for the crew and as in the case with the M24 the vehicle never got beyond the test stages.

The other anti-aircraft variant was the T100 which had four twenty millimeter cannons mounted in an enclosed turret. The turret was equipped with radar for target acquisition, one of the earliest attempts by the Army to provide radar control on a mobile anti-aircraft platform. Unfortunately problems with the radar and a lack of firepower led to cancellation of the project.

The other experimental vehicle was the T99, a modified chassis similar to the M44 and M52, which mounted a 155MM howitzer at the rear of the vehicle. This version was sometimes referred to as the "Austerity Mount" since the gun had neither a turret or armored superstructure. It was very much like the earlier M41 which had a similar arrangement on the hull of an M24 light tank. Unlike the M41, the T99 never went beyond the prototype stage, since the Army decided to use enclosed, revolving mounts for their self-propelled artillery.

In an attempt to provide a low cost self-propelled gun the T99 was developed as an alternative to the more costly variants fitted with enclosed revolving turrets. Similar to the earlier M41 (based on the M24 chassis) the T99 was often referred to as the "Austerity Mount." The chassis was very similar to the M44 and M52. (PAM)

The T100 was an experimental anti-aircraft vehicle based on the M41 which mounted four twenty millimeter cannons in a turret along with a self-contained radar unit for target acquisition and tracking. Problems with its light firepower and the radar, resulted in the project being cancelled. (PAM)

The driver's position on the T99 was just behind the engine compartment on the port side of 155 mm gun tube. The large springs at the rear of the gun barrel helped reduce recoil while the twin spades at the rear of the hull were used to dig the vehicle into position. (PAM)

Foreign Service

Over half of the total production of M41s were eventually supplied to various U.S. allies from the late 1950s onward. Over two dozen countries received the M41, either directly or indirectly as part of various American military aid programs. Because of its export to so many countries it was inevitable that it would see combat, although combat often involved their use by rebel forces in revolts against the various governments to which they had been supplied.

Perhaps the most famous of these actions was the use of the M41 by American backed Cuban refugees during the ill-fated Bay of Pigs invasion of 1961. Five M41s were landed to support the rebel brigade and, over the course of the battle, engaged a number of Cuban Army Soviet built T34/85s and SU-100s, emerging victorious on all occasions. When the invasion failed, the undamaged M41s were destroyed by their crews. Besides Cuba, M41s were a common sight in numerous coup attempts in the various Central and South American countries who received American military aid.

The M41 also saw combat service with a number of nations in Africa, the Middle East, and Asia. Prior to its shift toward the Soviet Union, M41s had made up the bulk of the Ethiopian armored force. After its shift into the Russian sphere of influence, T54/T55s were acquired to augment this force. The M41s eventually saw action alongside the Russian armor during fighting in the Ogaden Desert in northern Africa.

In the Middle East, Lebanon had a small fleet of M41s which served alongside French built AMX-13 light tanks. When the Lebanese Civil War began during 1975, the Lebanese Army virtually disappeared and much of its equipment fell into the hands of various warring factions. Whether or not any use was made of the M41s is unknown, although evidently no contact between them and the Israeli Army ever took place.

It was in South East Asia that the M41 saw most of its combat service. During the early 1960s American forces conducted a number of maneuvers in Thailand in response to communist moves in Laos and South Vietnam. These maneuvers also introduced U.S. troops to jungle and counter-insurgency warfare. To bolster its defenses Thailand received a number of M41s to replace its aging M24s. These vehicles were delivered under American treaty commitments as part of the SEATO agreement. These would see action in various clashes with communist backed insurgents along the Thai border with Laos and Cambodia and during coup attempts and civilian unrest in its major cities.

In South Vietnam, the Army of the Republic of Vietnam (ARVN) had been initially equipped with M5s and M24s after the French withdrawal from Vietnam during 1954. While the M5s were quickly discarded, the M24s continued to soldier on, but by the early 1960s, these were in need of replacement. In early 1965 as part of an increase in military aid, the U.S. began to supply ARVN armor/cavalry units with M41s. Their first significant action came during October of 1965, when an M41 squadron of fifteen tanks took part in the relief force assigned to raise the siege of the Plei Me Special Forces camp in the Central Highlands. Unfortunately, following this action, the American role in the war began to grow dramatically and the role of the ARVN forces decreased correspondingly.

The M41s, in particular, were hoarded near the cities and bases to protect high government or military officials and serve as a counter against possible coup attempts. Many armor officers received commands based on their politics rather than ability and this seriously affected the overall use and effectiveness of the tank units.

During the 1968 Tet Offensive, ARVN armor units played an important part in helping repulse the violent communist attacks against various cities and bases. The shock of this assault led to a revamping of the ARVN officer corps and, as a result, the armored units became less political in their makeup. They began to spend more time in the field and gained valuable combat experience. This became evident during the Cambodian invasion

The M41 saw extensive use in countries that had close military ties with the United States. Perhaps the largest users of the vehicle were members of NATO. A line of Belgium Army M41s wait to move out during an official function. (PAM)

A Danish tanker takes a break during maneuvers. This particular tank has the fittings for infrared searchlight on the port side of the main armament. (Turbridge via Foss)

of 1970 when ARVN armored units performed admirably alongside their American counterparts.

The first true test of the M41 in tank versus tank combat came during LAMSON 719, the ARVN invasion of Laos during 1971. Ground units, supported by three M41 squadrons, drove into Laos to cut the Ho Chi Minh trail near Aloiu and Tchepone. Initially the thrust met little opposition, but eventually the North Vietnamese moved in large numbers of men, tanks, and artillery to counter the ARVN attack. After forcing ARVN troops to retreat from two landing zones (LZ), a combined NVA tank-infantry team hit LZ31. Five M41s were detached to support this position and on 19 February the first major armor engagement of the war took place.

During the fight, the M41s, with supporting fire, destroyed six T54s and sixteen PT-76s without loss, but the NVA kept up their relentless assault on the position and eventually forced the ARVN troops to retreat. Buoyed by this success the NVA kept up the pressure on the ARVN force and the ARVN command decided to pull out. The retreat turned into a rout and when the ARVN forces finally reached the relative safety of South Vietnam, their losses had been staggering. Besides men, the ARVN forces lost large amounts of material including a number of M41s, some of which were put on display in Hanoi to celebrate the NVA victory.

Following LAMSON 719 each side drew back to lick their wounds. Unknown to U.S. and South Vietnamese officials the NVA was planning a massive conventional ground invasion of South Vietnam. This took place on 29 March 1972 when a massive tank-led assault, backed by a tremendous bombardment, pushed across the DMZ and overwhelmed a dozen ARVN fire support bases,. The few M41s in the area were unable to stop the large numbers of T54s, T59s, T34s, and PT-76s which rushed south toward Quang Tri and Da Nang. This advance was finally slowed by American air strikes and a hastily formed M48 tank regiment, which, in conjunction with the M41s finally held the line at the Meu Grang River near Dong Ha.

This line was eventually breached when additional NVA forces, equipped with wire guided Sagger anti-tank missiles, were able to flank the outnumbered ARVN forces. The ARVN forces retreated south of Quang Tri city which was abandoned to set up a new line. From this position, after being resupplied by the U.S. with additional equipment, including M41s, the ARVN forces launched a counterattack to recapture the lost ground. Backed by M41s, elite paratroop, Marine, and Ranger units retook Quang Tri. Due to their losses, however, they decided to consolidate their positions and wait before renewing their offensive.

Although not a member of NATO, and officially neutral, Austria has received American military aid, including a number of M41s. Austrian tanks carry a White triangle inside a Red circle as their national markings. (Wenzl via Jerchel)

An Austrian M41 moves across broken terrain during winter maneuvers. Austria received some forty early M41s as part of an American Military Assistance Program (MAP) aid package. (Austrian Army via Foss)

Beside the attack in the northern part of the country, the NVA also launched an offensive thrust in the Central Highlands toward Pleiku and Kontum and another in the south against Saigon. At Kotum a number of dug in M41s were systematically destroyed by Sagger missiles and artillery, while at An Loc, (north of Saigon) the defenders had no armor. At both places the NVA tanks were eventually defeated by a combination of M72 LAWs and air support. Relief columns, backed up by M41s, were finally able to break through the enemy lines and reinforce the areas, enabling the defenders to go on the offensive and drive the NVA forces back.

After the signing of the Paris Peace Accords in 1973, both sides again began to rebuild their strength for the final showdown. The South Vietnamese were hampered by American willingness to abide by the terms of the accords, while the North Vietnamese were under no such restrictions and built up their forces until they had a great advantage over the ARVN. While the Americans had poured large amounts of equipment, including M41s to replace material lost in 1972, gross mismanagement of this material, poor planning, and a lack of U.S. support led to a series of ARVN defeats during early 1975.

President Thieu issued a series of conflicting orders which resulted in the loss of many M41s, M48s and other armored vehicles. The NVA, pushing south along the coast, captured large numbers of M41s which had been abandoned for want of fuel and incorporated these into their own armored units. By mid-April the NVA was posed on the outskirts of Saigon for the final push. With the loss of so much of their armor, the South Vietnamese could do little to stop the communists, although a few ARVN tank units fought until the end at Loc Ninh and the approaches to Saigon.

Following their victory, the NVA incorporated a large number of captured M41s into their own units for use by occupation forces in the South. These were later used during the Vietnamese invasion of Cambodia and played an important part during the decade long war waged in the country until the Vietnamese withdrawal during the late 1980s. Some M41s may have been left behind to equip the Vietnamese installed Cambodian government, but little information is available on this. In all probability the M41s left in Vietnam continued to soldier on until a lack of spare parts forced their retirement.

In the Far East, a number of U.S. allies received M41s to bolster their defenses against communist aggression. Nationalist China received nearly 800 M41s, and was one of two countries that used every sub-type of the M41. This Chinese M41 takes part in a bridging exercise during maneuvers on Taiwan. (PAM)

Thailand was another country that used every sub-type of the M41, eventually receiving over 250 M41s during the 1960s and 1970s. Members of Troop B, 4th Cavalry, 25th Infantry Division, prepare their M41s to be turned over to the Thai Army. The Americans trained the Thai tankers in the operation of the light tank. (U.S. Army)

One of the first Thai units to received the M41 was the 6th Company. These vehicles are engaged in a road march to the firing range at Saraburi. The gun barrel was secured in place by the traveling lock on the rear of the hull. (U.S. Army)

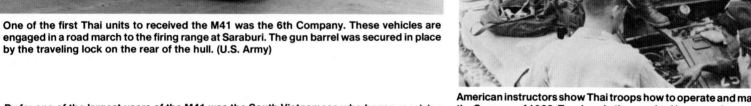

American instructors show Thai troops how to operate and maintain the M41's engine during the Summer of 1962. Tensions in the area had increased as a result of the war in Vietnam and the M41 proved to be an excellent tank to bolster Thai armored units as it was relatively simple and uncomplicated to operate and maintain. (U.S. Army)

By far one of the largest users of the M41 was the South Vietnamese who began receiving them during 1965. These M41s are from the 3rd ARVN Cavalry which helped support the South Korean Tiger Division near Pleiku in 1970. The sandbags tied to the turret are additional protection against enemy rocket propelled grenades (RPGs). (U.S. Army)

Besides RPGs, mines were also a major concern for ARVN tankers. This M41 ran over an aerial bomb which had been converted by the enemy into a land mine. The entire floor was blown in while most of the suspension on both sides was ripped away by the explosion. None of the crew survived. (Mesko)

The first major tank-versus-tank encounter of the Vietnam War occurred during LAMSON 719, the South Vietnamese invasion of Laos. This M41, piled high with extra machine gun ammo cans, moves along Colonial Route 9 during the drive to cut the Ho Chi Minh trail in Laos. (PAM)

Two ARVN M41s, camouflaged with vegetation and carrying extra ammo cans, move down Route 9 during the early part of LAMSON 719. Although there had been some minor armor battles earlier in the war, this offensive saw a number of battles between ARVN and NVA armor units. (U.S. Army)

During the Spring of 1972 the NVA launched a major ground attack against South Vietnam backed by large armored forces. M41s helped stem the initial onslaught in the northern province until additional forces could be brought to bear against the invaders. This ARVN M41 moves up toward Dong Ha in support of Vietnamese Marines. (U.S. Army)

At Dong Ha the ARVN forces held the NVA at bay for nearly a month until the ARVN flanks were turned. Two M41s sit behind dirt berms near Don Ha during a lull in the fighting. The berms provided additional protection from shells, RPGs, and wire guided anti-tank missiles. (U.S. Army)

A knocked-out ARVN M41A3 alongside the road to Quang Tri during the Spring of 1972. Due to the extensive fire damage, the armor integrity of the vehicle has probably been damaged beyond the point where the vehicle could be rebuilt. (Smock)

Numerous South American countries received M41s which were often used to help over throw their governments. These Argentine M41s take part in the annual military parade in the capital. The M41s were not used by the Argentine forces during the Falkland War. (Foss)

44

M41 Update Programs

Brazilian M41 Program

Brazil had received approximately 300 M41s under the Military Assistance Program (MAP) and during the early 1980s plans were drawn up to modernize these vehicles rather than purchase a new light tank. Part of the update would include the installation of a new power plant and heavier armament. The original 500 hp Continental or Lycoming gas engine was replaced with a Saab-Scania DS-14 diesel power plant which produced 400 horsepower. This new engine was much more fuel efficient and, as a result, the range of the M41 was nearly quadrupled (from 100 miles to 372 miles).

In place of the old 76MM gun, a new 90MM gun manufactured by Bernardini was fitted. This weapon was very similar to the Belgium Cockerill Mark III and could use the same range of ammunition. These modified tanks received the designation M41B and began to go into service with the Brazilian Army during the mid-1980s. A number of other countries expressed an interest in this conversion as a way of upgrading their aging M41 fleets.

Following this program, a new update package was developed by Bernardini. A more powerful engine replaced the Saab-Scani and armor side skirts were added for improved protection. While the same 90MM gun was retained, a new fire control system was added for improved target acquisition. This new vehicle received the designation M41C and consideration has been given to updating the earlier M41B conversions to M41C standards, but as yet this has not been implemented.

Cazador

Over the years the Spanish Army had received over 200 M41s. In an effort to upgrade these aging vehicles, the gas engines were replaced with the 450 hp GMC Detroit Diesel 8V-71T powerpack which increased their range from 100 miles to 347 miles. This was also the same engine which powered the M109 and M110 series of self-propelled guns. Additionally, plans were made to rearm half of the M41s for the anti-tank role, while the remainder were to retain their original 76MM cannon.

Initially two anti-tank guided missiles systems were tried, the Euromissile HCT turret armed with HOT ATGWs, and the Emerson Improved TOW (as fitted to the M901). After an extensive evaluation of both systems, the Spanish expressed an interest in the Emerson version.

Besides the new turret and engine, the basic M41 hull was extensively rebuilt with the forward portion of the hull being reworked to house the TOW mechanism, storage for ten additional missiles, fire control equipment and rearranged crew seating. The crew consisted of four, a commander, driver, gunner, and loader. Besides the missile system, the vehicle was also armed with a 7.62MM machine gun with 200 rounds for close in protection. The conversion work was carried out by Talbot of Spain and the name Cazador was given to the conversion of the M41.

Modernized M41

There have been a number of attempts by various U.S. and European firms to upgrade the M41 as an alternative to replacing the vehicle with a more costly new tank. The power plant, in particular, has been the focus of a great deal of this effort because of

Brazil converted a number of M41s to M41B standards by replacing the power plant with a Saab-Scania diesel engine and replacing the gun with a 90MM gun manufactured by Bernardini. These modified vehicles were more fuel efficient and allowed the useful life of the M41 to be extended. (Olive via Foss)

Following the work on the M41B Bernardini officials decided to modify the M41 further and added a more powerful engine, side skirts and an improved fire control system. This version of the M41 was designated the M41C. (Bernardini via Foss)

its poor fuel economy and short range. The U.S. firm of NAPCO developed a powerpack for the M41 based on the Detroit Diesel 450 hp 8V-71 diesel engine. Coupled to the original transmission, this engine nearly tripled the range of the M41 and a number of countries have shown an interest in the package. It is known that the re-engined vehicle was tested in Denmark, Spain and Thailand.

A Canadian company, Levy Autoparts, used the Cummings 500 horse power VTAk-903T diesel (the same engine used in the M2/M3 Bradley) as part of a conversion pack which increased the range by 250 percent (from 100 miles to 349 miles) while using the original transmission of the M41. Tests of this conversion were carried out in both Denmark and Thailand.

A similar conversion was also designed by FFG of West Germany, using the Rolls Royce Condor 550 hp CV-8 diesel engine (used in the MCV-80 Warrior, the British equivalent of the Bradley). As with the other conversions, this design also utilized the original transmission. Like the other conversions listed above, this conversion was also known to have been tested in both Denmark and Thailand.

Another area of the M41 which received attention was its armament. While still potent, it could not hope to match the new Soviet tanks. As a result, the Belgium firm of Cockerill fitted a MK IV 90MM low pressure gun in place of the 76MM cannon on an M41. The new gun greatly boosted the M41s firepower. The Mk IV fires a wide variety of ammunition, including HEAT-T, HE-T, HESH-T, Smoke-WP, and Canister. Uruguay, after viewing this conversion, decided to purchase twenty-four of the reconditioned vehicles to replace their aging M24 Chaffees.

In the U.S., tests were conducted with an M41 equipped with the British designed L-7 105MM low pressure cannon mounted in a Cadillac Gage Stingray turret to see if the weapon was suitable for use with the American Rapid Deployment Force (RDF). The system developed by Cadillac Gage was known as the Turret Modernization System and was designed to be installed by the receiving nation. The system gave the following advantages over a standard M41: improved low speed tracking, improved target acquisition, high precision gun positioning, improved first round hit capability, reduced system weight, simplified maintenance and operation, increased reliability and high systems growth potential.

American Army interest in this project never really developed as changing conditions and budgetary restraints hindered development of such a vehicle. Later events in Panama and the Persian Gulf have made U.S. officials acutely aware of the need for an effective light tank to replace the aging M551 Sheridan.

While the rearming of the M41 with such a large weapon was not contemplated for American forces, these tests did produce valuable information about the M41s ability to carry such armament. Due to the availability of such conversion packages, a number of countries have updated their M41s in various ways. Some programs have been relatively simple while others have resulted in an almost totally new vehicle. This has allowed the useful life of the M41 to be extended and undoubtedly these revamped M41s will see service into the 21st century, an amazing accomplishment for a vehicle designed shortly after the Second World War.

Plans were made to upgrade the earlier M41B conversions to M41C standards. This M41B has received side skirts and a camouflage paint scheme. Additional armor plating has been installed on the upper and lower portions of the front hull. (Olive via Foss)

Spanish interest in converting half of their M41 fleet to tank destroyers resulted in two prototype vehicles which mounted different anti-tank missile systems. This prototype mounted the Euromissile HCT turret with HOT ATGWs in a rotating turret. The hull was extensively rebuilt and a new power plant was fitted. (Talbot via Foss)

A more extensive conversion of the engine deck was required when the Ordnance Division of GTI/GLS modified the M41 with a more powerful and fuel efficient diesel engine. Additionally, smoke grenade launchers were added to the turret and a new turret storage box replaced the older one (GTI via Foss)

The other prototype mounted the Emerson Improved TOW system as used on the U.S. M901. This missile launcher, unlike the Euromissile one, was mounted in a retractable trunion which could be elevated when needed, keeping the vehicle profile low when the missile system was not in use. (Talbot via Foss)

The American firm of NAPCO designed a powerpack around the Detroit Diesel 8V-71T engine which nearly tripled the M41's old range. While basic hull remained much the same as the original the exhaust and muffler system was completely reworked. (NAPCO via Foss)

The solid engine access panels at the rear of the M41 were replaced with newer grated panels, which helped cool the engine compartment more efficiently and prevented engine overheating. (GTI via Foss)

The firm of Talbot modified the M41 using the NAPCO design along with other improvements such as the smoke grenade launchers on the turret sides. Internal changes also included improved first round hit probability and better communications. (Talbot via Foss)

The Belgian firm of Cockerill replaced the 76MM cannon with their low pressure 90MM Mark IV gun which significantly improved the firepower of the M41. The new cannon fires a wide variety of ammunition. The vehicle has been put into service with the Uruguyan Army. (PAM)

The M41 was used as a testbed for the Cadillac Gage LRF turret which mounted a British designed L-7 105мм gun. While not intended for production, the test vehicle showed the possibility of mounting such a modified gun on a light tank chassis. (Cadillac Gage via Foss)

A completely upgraded M41 currently in use by Denmark. This vehicle has received a new engine, upgraded sights and communications, grenade launchers, a revised turret storage basket, side skirts, infrared and searchlight capability and a new machine gun mount for the tank commander. (Foss)

2016

2022

2023

American Armor
from squadron/signal

2025

2026

2028